101

ESSENTIAL TIPS

Caring for Your
PET BIRD

ESSENTIAL TIPS

Caring for Your
PET BIRD

David Alderton

DK

DK PUBLISHING, INC.

A DK PUBLISHING BOOK

Editor Irene Lyford
Art Editor Martin Hendry
Series Editor Charlotte Davies
Series Art Editor Clive Hayball
Production Controller Lauren Britton
US Editor Laaren Brown

First American Edition, 1996
2 4 6 8 10 9 7 5 3
Published in the United States by DK Publishing, Inc.,
95 Madison Avenue, New York, New York 10016

Visit us on the World Wide Web at http://www.dk.com

ISBN 0-7894-1077-X

Text film output by The Right Type, Great Britain
Reproduced by Colourscan, Singapore
Printed and bound by Graphicom, Italy

ESSENTIAL TIPS

CHOOSING YOUR BIRD

1 WHICH SPECIES TO SELECT?

Before choosing a bird, look beyond its immediate appeal and think carefully about why you want one. Do you want a pet bird to keep in a cage indoors, or do you intend to build an outdoor aviary? Do you want a companion – a bird you can teach to talk, or one whose song will entertain you – or do you hope to breed and exhibit your birds?

◁ PARROTS & COCKATOOS
Young, hand-reared parrots can develop into superb pets as they are talented mimics and have a lifespan similar to humans. But they can be noisy and destructive, and housing these birds can be very expensive.

Sleek plumage indicates good health

YELLOW-FRONTED AMAZON PARROT

Blue cere (area above beak) distinguishes cock bird

GRAY-WINGED SKY BLUE BUDGERIGAR

Sky blue is palest blue shade

BUDGERIGARS ▷
Widely kept as companions, and popular as aviary and exhibition birds, budgerigars are available in a large range of varieties, from the pure snow-white albino to violets.

CRIMSON ROSELLA

◁ **PARAKEETS & COCKATIELS**
Although parakeets are ideal aviary birds, they are often too nervous to be good pets. Cockatiels, which share many of the attributes of budgerigars in terms of nature and mimicry, make better pets.

ST. HELENA WAXBILL

Wide tail feathers give rosellas their alternative name of "broadtails"

FINCHES ▷
Dainty and attractive, finches thrive in a planted aviary, where they often breed successfully. In colder climates, they may need extra heating in winter. Some finches are popular as exhibition birds.

SOFTBILLS ▽
This group comprises a wide range of birds, differing greatly in size. Most are aviary birds; certain species are social, but others need to be housed in individual pairs. They may feed on fruit, insects, nectar, and special softbill food and pellets.

RED-BILLED TOUCAN

Canary markings are highly individual

ROLLER CANARY

CANARIES ▷
The song of cock canaries has ensured their popularity as pets, but they can also be housed in a mixed aviary collection. Their colors range from pure white through reddish orange to dark green.

Toucans hold tail feathers vertically when roosting at night

9

*Evenly sized
nostrils free
of blockage
or erosion*

*Bright eyes
show no sign
of discharge
or swelling*

*Plump breast is well
covered with muscle*

COCKATOOS & PBFD
*Before buying a cockatoo,
check for stunted, twisted,
or brittle feathers, bald
areas, or changes in beak
shape or color – all signs
of PBFD (psittacine beak
and feather disease).*

*Glossy plumage,
with no noticeable
gaps or areas of
stunted growth*

*Toes correctly
positioned for
perching, with
no overgrown,
missing, or
deformed claws*

2 CHOOSING A HEALTHY BIRD

When choosing a bird, look first at its
general demeanor: one that appears
dull and unresponsive is unlikely to
be healthy. Then check for specific
points that can indicate problems.

- Check the nostrils for any discharge,
blockage, or signs of erosion.
- Examine the eyes for discharge or
swelling caused by blocked sinuses.
- Listen to the bird's breathing for
wheezing sounds, which can indicate
parasitic or fungal disease.
- Check the bill for deformities. With
budgies, check for scaly face mites.
- Check for slipped claws, which can
affect the bird's ability to perch.

MAROON-
BELLIED
CONURE

*Tail feathers intact,
neither soiled with
droppings at top nor
frayed at tips*

3 MALE OR FEMALE?

If you are looking for just one bird to keep as a pet indoors, you may wonder whether to get a cock or hen bird. Cocks are generally regarded as better pets as they are easier to tame and are not prone to the destructive behavior exhibited by hens at the start of the breeding period. If you want to teach your bird to talk, male birds are believed to be better mimics than females, although the latter can be trained.

Hen's plumage generally paler than male's

DNA SEXING
Using a blood sample, this is a reliable and safe way of sexing birds that cannot be sexed visually.

△ **SEXING A BUDGIE**
The sex of an adult budgerigar is evident from the color of its cere (the area above the beak); it is blue or purple in a cock, brown in a hen.

△ **PAIR OF CUT-THROAT FINCHES**
Here the cock is clearly distinguished by red throat markings and darker plumage.

4 TWO'S COMPANY

Although a single bird is easier to tame, and is likely to be a better companion, you may prefer to get a pair of birds who will provide company for each other if you are often out of the house. In this case, it is best to get two young birds at the same time, but to train them as individuals. Two cocks are less likely to quarrel than two females.

5 ADVANTAGES OF A HAND-REARED CHICK

Hand-reared chicks, and chicks whose nestboxes are cleaned regularly, are easier to train since they are accustomed to human company. Young birds generally adapt quickly to new situations, but adults are often nervous and shy, and are unlikely ever to form close bonds with people.

6 HOW TO TELL YOUR BIRD'S AGE

Iris coloration provides a good indication of age in many birds: a young budgie's eyes lack the white irises that become evident at 12 weeks. A young budgerigar is also distinguished by fine black bars on its forehead, which vanish at the first molt, again around 12 weeks. Adult budgies have a well-defined mask, with larger spots.

Barring extends over forehead; ill-defined "mask"

Clear forehead, and large, round spots forming "mask"

SIX-WEEK-OLD CHICK   ADULT BUDGIE

IRIS COLORATION ▷
The difference in iris coloration between the young African Gray Parrot (above) and its four-year-old parent is a useful guide to the ages of the two birds.

Pale yellowish iris indicates adult bird

7 CHECKING FOR BILL DEFORMITIES

Uncorrected bill deformities may cause eating difficulties. An under-shot bill needs regular trimming, but an overgrown bill may be improved by providing the bird with suitable wood for gnawing.

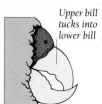

Upper bill tucks into lower bill

UNDERSHOT BILL
IN BUDGIE

OVERGROWN UPPER
BILL IN BUDGIE

8 OVERGROWN CLAWS

Although not a serious defect, overgrown claws need trimming to prevent a bird getting caught up in the cage bars or aviary wire netting. Nuns and weavers often have long, straggling claws, and canaries and budgerigars also need to have their claws trimmed regularly.

NORMAL CLAW   HOOKED CLAW

SPINDLY CLAW   CURLED CLAW

CHOOSING YOUR BIRD

⑨ CHECKING FOR WING & TAIL DAMAGE

Although the state of a bird's plumage is not a very good clue to its general condition, it is vital to check the wing and tail feathers of a budgerigar before purchase, to avoid selecting birds with "French molt," a viral disease that leads to feather loss. Gaps in the flight and tail feathers of young birds usually indicate French molt.

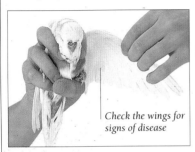

Check the wings for signs of disease

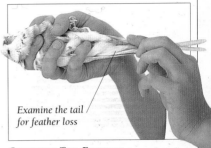

Examine the tail for feather loss

EXAMINE THE WINGS FOR DAMAGE
Gaps in the wing feathers of a young bird, and dried blood in the feather shafts of an older bird, both indicate French molt.

CHECK THE TAIL FEATHERS
Besides checking that the tail feathers are intact, look for staining around the vent, which could indicate digestive problems.

⑩ HOW TO TELL A SICK BIRD

It is fairly easy to spot a sick bird as its demeanor is so different from the usual bright, lively behavior. A sick bird hunches up with its feathers fluffed out and its eyes closed. It sleeps a lot, with its head tucked in, and seems dull and dejected compared to its healthy companions.

Bird sleeps longer than usual

Plumage around bill may be stained

Weight loss evident over breastbone

Wings often droop at sides of body

Sick bird is unsteady on its feet

EMERGENCY TREATMENT
Whatever the cause, a sick bird loses body heat rapidly, often with fatal consequences, so transfer it to a warm environment and seek help.

HOUSING & EQUIPMENT

11 SELECTING THE BEST CAGE FOR YOUR BIRD

Your choice of cage depends on which birds you intend to keep in it, but it must be big enough to allow a bird to fly between the perches. For birds with long tails, such as macaws, a taller cage is needed. Make sure that the door fastens securely and, if necessary, clamp food and water dishes in place. Replace plastic perches with natural wooden ones, which will be more comfortable for your bird.

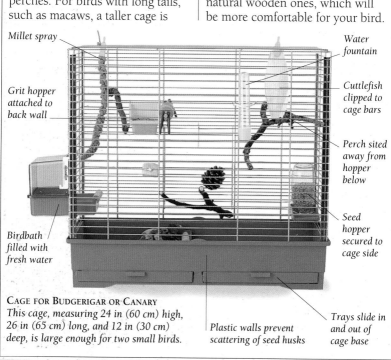

Millet spray

Grit hopper attached to back wall

Birdbath filled with fresh water

Water fountain

Cuttlefish clipped to cage bars

Perch sited away from hopper below

Seed hopper secured to cage side

CAGE FOR BUDGERIGAR OR CANARY
This cage, measuring 24 in (60 cm) high, 26 in (65 cm) long, and 12 in (30 cm) deep, is large enough for two small birds.

Plastic walls prevent scattering of seed husks

Trays slide in and out of cage base

12 VARY THE CAGE-FLOOR COVERING

Many materials are available for covering the floor of a cage, and it is a good idea to vary these from time to time. Gravel paper for birds is convenient as droppings can be scraped off and the sheets renewed just once or twice a week. Bird sand or corncob is inexpensive and provides minerals and grit, but must be changed more frequently.

LINING PAPER

GRAVEL PAPER

Lining paper is a cheap covering

BIRD SAND　　**WOOD SHAVINGS**

PLASTIC BASE COVER
An elasticized plastic cover around the base of a bird cage will help keep the surrounding area clean.

13 WHERE TO PLACE YOUR CAGE

Although finches or softbills should be kept in a quiet room with minimal disturbance, pet birds should be kept in the living area of your house, in a room that can be adapted to minimize risks.
- Place the cage at eye-level height, where you can talk to the bird and let it feed from your hand.
- Support the cage on a secure stand or on a piece of furniture.
- Don't put the cage in the kitchen, where toxic fumes may prove fatal.
- Keep the cage away from bright sunlight and drafts.
- Make sure that cats and other pets cannot reach the cage.

14 WHEN TO USE A PET CARRIER

A plastic pet carrier is useful, not just for taking a larger bird to the vet or to shows, but for temporary accommodation while cleaning the main cage. Put your bird in it also to give it a refreshing shower.

Check size of mesh before using for smaller birds

Cover floor of carrier with lining paper before use

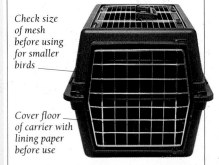

15 COVERING THE CAGE

Your pet bird will rest more soundly if you exclude light from its cage, so cover the cage at night and when the bird is resting after its free-exercise period. During the daytime, cover the corner of the cage with the highest perch so that the bird can rest in a darkened area when it is tired.

ALLOW FOR A DAYTIME REST

16 WHY A NATURAL PERCH IS BEST

Birds need to gnaw on wood and bill deformities may result if this need is thwarted. You can cut perches from nonpoisonous trees or bushes: select a suitable branch, at least ½ in (10 mm) wide, wash it, and trim it to fit the perch holder provided in the bird cage.

17 SELECTING SUITABLE TOYS

When choosing toys for your pet bird, remember that they will have to be kept clean, so the simpler they are, the better. Check for sharp edges and ensure that toxic paint has not been used. Simple items, such as a wooden thread spool or a Ping-Pong ball, make excellent toys for birds.

A piece of doweling makes a good toy for this lory

WOODEN BALL

PINE CONE

Budgies enjoy swinging and scampering up and down ladders

18 MAKING YOUR ROOM SAFE

A bird needs regular free exercise, but make sure the room is safe.

- Close windows and cover glass with curtains or screening.
- Screen the fireplace and place guards around other heaters.
- Ensure that cats and dogs are excluded from the room.
- Check that plants are not toxic.
- Do not leave hot drinks unattended.

BORN TO FLY
For birds such as this Blue & Gold Macaw, regular free exercise is vital.

◁ **SAFETY FIRST**
Before your bird is let loose in a room, cover the windows with fine netting to keep it from flying into the glass. Place a screen over the fireplace too.

FINE NETTING

PLANTS TO AVOID
Some houseplants, such as Amaryllis, Philodendron, and Diffenbachia, are poisonous to birds when eaten.

19 RETURNING A BIRD TO ITS CAGE

CATCHING AN ESCAPED BIRD

Encourage your bird to return to its cage after its exercise period by leaving the cage door open and putting some fresh food in the tray. If it is reluctant to return to the cage, or if it escaped for any reason, draw the curtains, turn off all the lights in the room, then gently place a dustcloth over the bird. Pick it up in the cloth, then place the bundle in the cage. Let your bird rest after its exertions.

20 KEEPING BIRDS IN AN AVIARY

An outdoor aviary provides the opportunity to develop your interest in birdkeeping, to build up a collection of whichever birds take your fancy, and to become involved in breeding and rearing stock. A typical aviary consists of the mesh flight, which is partially open to the elements; a shelter, where the birds feed and roost; and a safety porch to ensure that birds cannot escape as you enter.

HANGING HOPPER

OPEN SEED TRAY

LARGE MINERAL BLOCK

GRIT TRAY

AVIARY EQUIPMENT △
In addition to a large seed hopper, you will need several trays for grit, seed, and other foodstuffs. Put drinking water in a sealed water fountain to keep it clean.

Shelter has perches inside for birds to roost

21 SITING YOUR AVIARY

When planning an aviary, think carefully about its location.
- First, check whether any local regulations might apply.
- Look for a level, sheltered site that can be seen from the house.
- Find a site where the birds will not disturb your neighbors.
- Avoid a site close to the road where birds could be disturbed by car headlights, noise, or vandals.
- Ensure that there are no overhanging trees whose branches could damage the structure.

Timber frame treated with nontoxic preservative

Natural wooden perches provide opportunities for gnawing

Seed dish, preferably hung inside shelter

Entrance to aviary is via safety porch

Floor slopes away from shelter for good drainage

Openings in mesh no larger than 1 x ½ in (2.5 x 1.25 cm)

AVIARY FLOOR
The aviary will be easier to clean and disinfect if you cover the floor with tiles or concrete.

22 AVIARY PLANTS

Shrubs provide dense cover and nesting sites for small birds, while annuals such as nasturtiums (*Tropaeolum majus*) add color and attract insects. Grow plants in tubs, which can be easily moved to clean the aviary.

Remove annuals in autumn when the blooms die

23 WHICH BIRDS FOR THE AVIARY?

All the birds featured in this book can be housed in an aviary for at least part of the year, if you live in a temperate region. Some species will need additional lighting and warmth during the winter.

COCK

HEN

Golden-breasted Waxbills may require extra heating in winter

HANDLING YOUR BIRD

24 GETTING YOUR BIRD HOME

Airholes in top of box

Be sure to take a suitable container with you when you go to buy a bird. A cardboard box, with airholes punched in it, is suitable for small birds; for larger birds, you will need something more substantial, such as a plywood box with a hinged lid for easy access.

CARDBOARD CARRYING BOX

25 HOW TO HANDLE SMALL BIRDS

To catch a bird in a cage, wait until it comes to rest on the floor, then gently place your hand over it. As soon as its wings are closed, close your hand around it, then slowly withdraw your hand from the cage. Hold its neck between your first and second fingers, with its wings restrained in the palm of your hand.

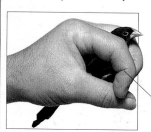

ALTERNATIVE HOLD ▷
If you prefer, hold your bird cupped in both hands – but this is not recommended for birds that bite.

Hold the bird firmly but be careful not to squeeze its neck

26 PRECAUTIONS WHEN HANDLING PARROTS

It is best to wear gloves when handling parrots as they may bite, but be careful not to apply too much pressure. When handling very large species, such as macaws, wear a thinner pair of gloves beneath a thick outer pair. If a parrot does bite, just loosen your grip slightly – you should be able to restrain it again before it flies off.

SAFELY RESTRAINED ▷
Once a parrot is restrained it will usually stop struggling and allow you to carry out an examination or clip its claws.

27 HANDLING HINTS

Before removing a bird from its cage, check that all doors and windows in the room are closed.

- Take out any food containers or perches that could obstruct easy removal of the bird from the cage.
- If the bird shows signs of distress, such as panting heavily, leave it until it has recovered.
- Do not try to catch aviary birds during the hottest part of the day; the heat puts additional stress on birds.
- If wearing thick gloves, be careful not to squeeze too hard.

28 INTRODUCING NEW BIRDS

Prepare for the arrival of new birds by making sure that the housing is clean and equipped before bringing them home. Try to obtain a diet plan from the previous owner so that you can stock up on the same food. Always isolate the newcomers for a period to make sure that they are not incubating a disease, and to enable you to carry out treatment against parasites.

◁ **PREVENT BULLYING**
Check regularly on newcomers to the aviary to ensure that no bullying occurs.

29 MAKING CONTACT

Allow new birds a few days to adjust before starting training, then try to establish a regular routine. Build up the bird's confidence gradually, and repeat each step until it is used to it, before going on to the next stage.

△ **FEELING SECURE**
Once a budgie is used to you, it will sit happily on your finger, gripping it with his claws.

1 △ Begin to get your budgie used to your hand by pushing a piece of its favorite fresh food through the cage bars.

2 △ When it is used to your presence, put your hand in the cage and gently stroke its neck while it is eating.

TABLE MANNERS
Never let your parrot out of its cage at mealtimes; not only will it make a nuisance of itself, trying to steal from your plate, but it may eat unsuitably salty or fatty food.

3 ◁ Attach a piece of fresh food to a perch and slowly move it toward your budgie. It will gradually feel secure enough to step onto the perch.

Attach food to perch with clip

30 CREATING A BOND

With patience and kindness you can build a strong rapport with a tame bird. Having gained its confidence, set aside a regular time each day for training sessions. Never punish your pet, as this will harm the bond between you.

Tame parrot enjoys being tickled on back of head

31 TEACH YOUR BIRD TO TALK

Teaching a bird to talk is essentially a matter of patience and repetition, and of breaking sentences and words into short phrases. Birds generally find it easier to mimic a woman's or child's voice rather than a man's. Have several training sessions a day, making sure that the surroundings are quiet. Listen for words or phrases in the bird's chatter and repeat these back to him.

NATURAL MIMIC ▷
The African Gray Parrot is said to be the best natural mimic, though Mynah birds have better diction.

32 BIRDS FOR CHILDREN

Budgerigars, deservedly popular as children's pets, are lively, easy to look after, and highly adaptable. Budgerigars are also naturally tame and safe for children to handle, and they are talented mimics.

YOUNG COMPANIONS

33 YOUR BIRD & OTHER PETS

It is safest never to let your bird out of its cage when another pet is in the room. Make sure, too, that the cage cannot be knocked over by a boisterous dog; place it on a piece of furniture rather than on a stand.

Good friends – but don't take chances

23

FEEDING YOUR BIRDS

34 CHOOSING THE RIGHT BIRD FOOD

Seed forms a major part of many birds' diets. It can be divided into two main groups: cereals, such as canary seed, which are high in carbohydrates; and oil-based seeds, such as sunflower, pine nuts, and peanuts, which also have a higher protein content. Most species of birds have preferences for particular kinds of seeds, and this is reflected in the seed mixtures available from pet stores. Budgerigar seed mixture usually consists of canary seed and millet, but different types of millet are available and some are more appealing to budgies than others. Parrots prefer a mixture that is high in oil seed, although they are now being fed on complete food mixes,

MILLET SPRAY

Birds enjoy pecking seeds from millet spray

BUDGERIGAR MIX

CANARY MIX

FOREIGN FINCH MIX

SOAKING SEED
Soaking seed in hot water for 24 hours increases protein content and makes it more digestible for chicks and convalescent birds.

BLUE MAW (POPPY SEED)

NIGER

SEED HOPPER △
Every day, remove husks from the hopper and refill with seed as necessary.

35 THE NEED FOR DAILY FRUIT

Many birds need a daily selection of fruit, the choice depending on local availability. Make sure that the fruit has no mold or bruised areas, and always wash it first as a precaution against any chemical residues. Peel oranges and remove peach pits and other large seeds. Introduce new fruits gradually to limit risk of digestive problems.

COMPLETE FOOD
(CANARIES & FINCHES)

COMPLETE FOOD
(LARGE PARROTS)

ORANGE

POMEGRANATE

SOFTBILL FOOD

PARROT FOOD

DRIED APRICOT

CHERRIES

APPLE

Apples are popular with birds; avoid damaged fruit

PINE NUTS

PEANUTS

RASPBERRIES

36 SELECTING SUITABLE VEGETABLES

Vegetables are an important source of nutrients for birds, so provide a fresh selection every day. Spinach is a valuable source of vitamin A, some of the B vitamins, and minerals such as iron. Offer cabbage leaves or stalks to your parrot in winter, but these may not be readily eaten by budgerigars. Sprouting seeds are nutritious and popular with parrots. However, you must check sprouts before offering them to make sure that they are fresh and not moldy.

TOMATOES

ALFALFA

SPINACH

PEAS

CARROT

CELERY

FREEZING SUPPLIES
Freeze corn on the cob when in season and keep for later use.

37 WHICH LIVE FOODS?

Although canaries, parrots, and budgerigars need a basic diet of only seed, fruit, and vegetables, other species benefit greatly from eating live insect food. This is particularly important with many softbills and finches, especially when breeding, since the increased amount of protein obtained from live food helps them to sustain the rapid growth of their chicks. Mealworms are the most popular live food for birds, but you might consider breeding a stock of crickets or locusts, which are good sources of protein, although low in calcium.

LOCUST NYMPHS

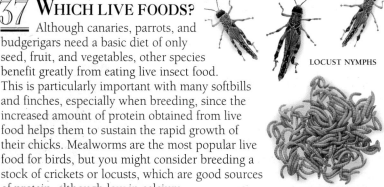

MEALWORMS

38 SUPPLEMENTING THE BASIC DIET

In addition to grit, birds that are regularly fed on seed should be provided with cuttlefish bone, which is a valuable source of calcium. Make sure that the softer, powdery side of the bone is accessible to the birds. Budgerigars should also be given an iodine block to ensure healthy thyroid activity. Vitamin supplements are available but, before using them, assess your bird's diet carefully to determine whether it is likely to be deficient in anything.

PARROT
CHEW
RING

CHARCOAL

RED PEPPER

IODINE BLOCK

MINERAL
GRIT

OYSTER SHELL
GRIT

POWDERED VITAMIN
SUPPLEMENT

CUTTLEFISH
BONE

39 THE IMPORTANCE OF GRIT

Grit not only provides minerals in a bird's diet, but plays an important part in the digestive process of seed-eating birds. Birds have no teeth, and grit helps to grind up whole food in the gizzard before it is broken down by enzymes and absorbed through the intestinal wall.

Grit hopper
hooks onto bird cage

40 PROVIDE THE RIGHT DIET FOR YOUR BIRD

Most birds feed constantly throughout the day, so ensure that a supply of food is always available.

Consult the chart below for a quick guide to the feeding requirements of different groups of birds.

Bird group	Main food	Other requirements
Finches	Plain canary seed and mixed millets. Some species may also eat rape, niger, and blue maw (poppy seed)	Green food such as seeding grasses, finely chopped chickweed, dandelion, or spinach. Live food is very important for many species, particularly during the breeding season
Canaries	Plain canary seed, rape seed, hemp, niger, and blue maw. Also weed seeds if available	Green food and egg food, which is especially important when chicks are being reared. Color-feeding (see p.33) is also necessary for some breeds being bred for exhibition purposes
Softbills	Fruit such as apples and grapes, plus softbill food or pellets and invertebrates. Some also require nectar	You may need to cut fruit into small pieces for many species. Low-iron softbill food recommended in many cases to avoid iron storage disease. Provide fresh food every day
Budgerigars	Mixture of millets and plain canary seed	Offer groats and soft food, especially during the breeding period. Green food will be readily consumed, and carrots may be accepted, but the juice of the latter may stain the facial feathering
Cockatiels & Parakeets	Millets, plain canary seed, groats, sunflower seed, small pine nuts, and peanuts, or a complete food	Proportions depend on the species concerned; those of Australian origin require a cereal-based diet, composed of a higher proportion of millets and plain canary seed. Green food is also needed, as well as fruit
Parrots & Cockatoos	Good quality parrot seed mixture, including sunflower seed, groats, flaked maize, and peanuts. Complete foods also available	Smaller species, such as lovebirds and parrotlets, will eat mainly millets and canary seed. Nectar is the main food of lories and lorikeets, and should also be offered to hanging parrots. Offer fruit and green food daily

41 THE IMPORTANCE OF FRESH WATER

Make sure that your birds always have fresh water to drink, replacing water in the fountain daily, or more often if necessary. Prevent the water becoming contaminated by using a sealed fountain that releases a small amount at a time, and by ensuring that water containers are not placed beneath perches. In winter, check drinking fountains each morning in case ice has formed in the spouts.

CLEAN WATER SUPPLY
Drinking water is kept clean in enclosed tube until required, with only small quantity being allowed through into trough.

Bird sits on perch below fountain

42 FOOD DISHES & HOPPERS

Plastic containers, which are cheap, easy to clean, and available in a range of sizes, are perfect for smaller, nondestructive species. However, you will have to provide metal containers for parrots. Use smaller containers for soaked seed, and larger ones for fruit, vegetables, and live foods.

◁ **GRIT HOPPER**

Grit hopper attaches to cage with rear hook

◁ **AIRTIGHT CONTAINER**

Keep bird seed fresh in airtight plastic container

Base of hopper provides feeding perch

SEED HOPPER

43 TEACHING YOUNG BIRDS TO FEED

Without a more experienced bird to imitate, a young bird that is housed alone may have difficulty in feeding from a covered hopper. Encourage it by sprinkling a little seed on the floor around the base of the pot. To help a bird learn to drink from an enclosed water container, dip the tip of its bill in the water for a few seconds.

HYGIENE & HEALTH CARE

44 ESSENTIAL CLEANING EQUIPMENT

Although you need little more than standard household items for cleaning bird cages and aviaries, make sure that these are kept separately and used only for this purpose. Choose appropriate disinfectants, making sure that they are not toxic to birds. Always rinse the cage and other equipment with clean water after disinfecting.

△ BOTTLE BRUSH

SCRUB BRUSH △

DETERGENT SPONGE SCRAPER RUBBER GLOVES DISINFECTANT

45 DAILY CLEANING ROUTINE

It is very important for your bird's health that its cage and equipment are kept scrupulously clean. Every day, scrape out any dirty litter from the floor tray and replace the floor covering if necessary. Remove any empty seed husks from the hopper and, after cleaning, refill the water container with fresh water.

FRESH FOOD TRAY ▷
Every day, prepare a tray of fresh fruit and vegetables, cut into chunks, and place it on the cage floor.

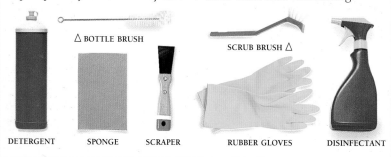

46 KEEP YOUR BIRD'S CAGE CLEAN

Once a week, put your birds into a temporary accommodation, such as a spare cage or a pet carrier, while you clean their cage and equipment. Take out all perches, dishes, and food containers, and dispose of food, water, and dirty floor coverings. Remove any cuttlefish or iodine block from the bars of the cage.

Clean all around cage bars with hot soapy water

△ **DISPOSE OF DIRTY LITTER**
Use a scraper to remove any dirty litter from the floor trays.

△ **CLEAN THE CAGE**
Wash the cage with hot soapy water, disinfect, rinse, then let dry. Scrub, disinfect, and rinse the perches, hoppers, and floor trays, and replace when dry.

DISINFECTANTS
Bleach is a commonly used disinfectant, but other disinfectants are also recommended for washing out cages.

△ **WASH & DISINFECT TRAYS**
Scrub trays with hot soapy water; disinfect, rinse, then let dry.

△ **CLEAN OUT WATER CONTAINER**
Thoroughly clean and rinse the fountain, using a bottlebrush to reach the end of the tube.

47 PROVIDE A BATH FOR YOUR BIRD

Regular bathing is essential for birds kept indoors, helping to keep their plumage healthy and lessening the risk of feather-plucking. While a budgerigar will happily bathe in a saucer of water, it is a good idea to provide a special birdbath, with enclosed sides. Your bird can then splash around as much as he wants without creating too much mess. Provide a shallow bowl of water for aviary birds to bathe in, changing the water frequently.

Bathing helps keep feathers in good condition

Birdbath with splash hood hooks over cage-door opening

CUSTOMIZED BIRDBATH
Make sure that this birdbath, which hooks over the cage door opening, is securely attached, otherwise the bird may escape.

△ **BATHING IN A SAUCER**
When your bird is out of the cage, let it bathe in a shallow bowl of water, protecting the floor with plastic sheeting.

BATHING PREFERENCES
Fill the birdbath with tepid tap water. Change the water and clean the bath after it has been used, as birds will not bathe in dirty water. If you like, add a little feather conditioner to the water.

48 SPRAYING FOR HEALTHY PLUMAGE

Many parrots prefer a shower to bathing in a bowl of water, and, if you keep such birds indoors, you will have to spray them regularly. Do this just before you clean their cage, when food containers have been removed. Use a plant sprayer, setting it to give a fine, mistlike spray. Direct the spray so that the water droplets fall lightly on the bird from above; never point it directly at the bird as this is likely to upset it.

PLANT SPRAYER

49 WHY BIRDS PREEN & MOLT

Preening is an important activity for a healthy bird, serving not just to groom the plumage and to remove the sheaths of new feathers as they emerge, but also to spread oil from the preen-gland (which is located just above the base of the tail) to the feathers – a vital factor in keeping the bird waterproof.

During molting, the bird loses its old feathers, which are then replaced by a new set. It is a normal phenomenon that occurs about once a year – although this varies from one species to another. Molting ensures that the bird's ability to fly and to withstand the elements is adequately maintained.

Preening is a bird's way of grooming itself

ROLLER CANARY

Bird spreads oil from preen-gland over feathers

COLOR-FEEDING
Color-feeding is a means of enhancing the coloration of certain birds. To color-feed, add a coloring agent to the bird's water or its food, just before the molting period begins.

50 SHOWING YOUR BIRD

If you are interested in showing your birds, start by visiting as many bird shows as possible; these provide a good opportunity to see how the birds are presented and judged. Find out the standards for the varieties you are interested in; these establish the ideal characteristics for each variety. Shows are advertised in specialized birdkeeping magazines, which are another good source of information.

A WINNING PAIR OF ZEBRA FINCHES

51 THE IMPORTANCE OF EXERCISE

Long primary flight feathers

PRINCESS OF WALES' PARAKEET

Shorter secondary feathers

A pet bird needs regular exercise outside the cage. Set aside a time each day when you are free for half an hour to supervise the session. Your bird will want to rest during its exercise period, so provide some perches around the room, laying newspaper underneath to prevent any mess.

Tail feathers vary in length

FLYING GEAR
A bird's flying ability depends to a large extent on the feathers on its wings and tail. Each type of feather serves a specific function.

52 LOOKING AFTER YOUR BIRD'S FEET

Various diseases can be spread from fecal contamination of a bird's feet, so make sure that they are kept clean. If soiling does occur, soak the bird's feet in tepid water for a minute or two before trying to remove the dirt, but be careful not to damage the skin. Apply some germicidal ointment afterward as a preventive measure.

Blood supply to claw visible under bright light. Cut beyond end of this area

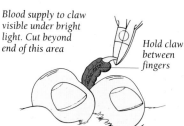

Hold claw between fingers

WHEN TO CLIP A BIRD'S CLAWS
If the claws become overgrown, they will curl around, causing perching problems. Cut them back with a pair of clippers if necessary.

53 VACATION CARE

Whether you intend to take your pet bird to stay with a friend while you are on vacation, or have arranged for someone to come in to tend to your aviary, make sure that everything is well organized.

- Leave enough of all types of food, grit, floor coverings, and cleaning materials, all clearly labeled.
- Leave clear, written instructions detailing everything that needs to be done each day and week.
- If you have several pairs of birds in an aviary, number their bands so that there is no confusion.
- Leave details of your vet's name, address, and telephone number.

54 SEASONAL REQUIREMENTS

When extra heating is required in the bird room or in an outdoor aviary, the safest option is a sealed tubular heater, combined with a thermostat for economy. Be sure that all electrical wiring and apparatus is fully shielded from the birds.

Finches often need additional heating and light in winter

55 FIRST AID FOR YOUR BIRD

Accidents may befall your pet birds, so be ready for the most common emergencies.

- If a bird gets caught in the aviary mesh, restrain it with one hand while you free its claw, trying not to distress it further.
- If you rescue a bird from a cat, take it to the vet if the skin is broken; otherwise, leave it to recover quietly in its cage.
- If you find a disoriented bird on the floor of the aviary, place it in a box in a quiet place where it can rest comfortably. If the wings are damaged, take it to the vet.
- Stem bleeding with a styptic pencil; if bleeding is extensive, apply pressure. If the tongue is involved, take the bird to the vet.

NAIL CLIPPERS

ANTI-MITE SPRAY

COTTON SWABS

STYPTIC PENCIL

BIRD AID
Make up a first-aid kit to deal with emergencies.

56 WHEN TO CONSULT A VET

The condition of a sick bird usually deteriorates rapidly, so seek medical help without delay. Describe to the vet the bird's symptoms, along with details of its history and diet, and whether any of your other birds are affected. Your vet will advise you about the availability of vaccinations against certain diseases.

PROFESSIONAL ADVICE

57 BEHAVIORAL PROBLEMS

Behavioral problems in birds commonly occur as sexual maturity approaches. At this time, a cock budgerigar may start "feeding" toys in the cage or try to mate with them, while the hen bird becomes broody and may lay eggs on the floor of the cage. A parrot's desire to breed is often indicated by aggression, while cockatoos display frequently, call loudly, and may become destructive.

△ FEATHER-PLUCKING
This major behavioral problem in parrots is difficult to deal with unless the underlying reason is discovered. Boredom is often cited as a factor.

Upright stance indicates dominant posture

Partially open wings serve as a threat gesture

YELLOW-STREAKED LORY

HOW TO PREVENT PROBLEMS
- *Start with a young bird, and buy two if you are often away.*
- *Spray your bird regularly.*
- *Offer a balanced diet.*
- *Provide branches to gnaw on.*

58 COMMON HEALTH PROBLEMS

While it is fairly easy to spot a sick bird, it is more difficult to identify what is wrong with it. Birds deteriorate very rapidly when ill, however, so early diagnosis is vital. Inspect your birds every day in order to spot any problems as early as possible. If you discover a sick bird, move it to a warm atmosphere, at least 86° F (30° C), as birds lose heat rapidly when they are not eating, and the resulting hypothermia can prove fatal.

EARLY SCALY FACE
Scaly face, shown here by tiny tracks across the bird's upper bill, results from mite infestation.

Major health problems associated with bird species

Bird group	What to watch for	Action
Finches	Overgrown claws	Arrange to clip claws back
	Soiling around vent	Indicates digestive disorder; antibiotics may be required
Canaries	Swelling, which could be feather cysts	Alter breeding program
	Persistent preening	Treat for mites or lice
Softbills	Aggressive behavior at start of breeding period	Remove cock bird for a time, and trim his flight feathers to prevent injury to hen
	Swollen abdomen; some difficulty in flying	Suggestive of iron storage disease. Modify diet; avoid dry fruits
Budgerigars	Green droppings	Antibiotic therapy may be needed
	Swollen crop and retching.	Treat for trichomoniasis
	Coral-like growths around beak	Treat scaly face with commercial remedy or ivomectin
	Chicks lose flight feathers – French molt	Viral illness; disinfect quarters thoroughly. No treatment available
Cockatiels & Parakeets	Loss of condition; chicks may die soon after fledging. White roundworms visible in droppings	Deworm birds and disinfect aviary to kill worm eggs here, which could reinfect the birds
Parrots & Cockatoos	Feather loss, flaking of bill and claws	Arrange test for PBFD. Infectious, and no treatment available. Keep affected birds strictly isolated

BIRD BREEDING

59 PREPARATION FOR BREEDING

Some birds prefer to build their own nests among the shrubs in the aviary, while others have to be provided with the appropriate nestbox, basket, nest pan, or nesting material. Exhibition birds, however, are usually bred in specially designed breeding cages, so that the parentage of the chicks can be controlled. These cages are available in various sizes and materials; metal is the most durable and easiest to clean, but also the most expensive. Plywood is a cheaper option.

CANARY
NEST PAN

Do not disturb nesting birds

NESTING EQUIPMENT ▷
Encourage breeding activity by providing a good range of possible nest sites and nest-building material appropriate to the birds concerned.

HORIZONTAL FINCH NESTING BASKET

NESTING BOX FOR FINCH OR SMALL SOFTBILL

NESTING BOX FOR PARROT OR PARAKEET

NESTING MATERIAL ▷
Make sure that all nesting material provided is sterile and that it presents no hazard to the birds. Dried moss, a popular nest liner, is available from florists.

NESTING FIBER

COCONUT FIBER

60 HATCHING & REARING

Note the date when egg-laying begins, so that you can assess when the eggs are likely to hatch; bear in mind that the incubation period may not start until the second or third egg has been laid. (Watch for signs of egg-binding, a serious condition in which the hen will appear ill, become unsteady on her feet, and be unable to perch.) Toward the end of the incubation period, start offering small quantities of rearing food.

△ **INCUBATION**
Budgerigars' eggs hatch after 18 days.

△ **WEANING**
Place a dish of soaked seed and diced fruit on the floor of the cage to encourage chicks to start feeding independently. Also provide fresh water.

Allow plenty of time for feeding chicks

△ **HEALTHY BILLS**
Regularly check inside the mouths of very young budgerigars, as any dirt here may lead to distortion of the bill.

◁ **HAND-REARING**
Use a teaspoon or glass dropper to feed the chicks, gradually increasing the interval between feedings from every two to every four hours.

61 BANDING YOUR BIRD

A bird cannot be entered in a breeder's class at a show without the proper band, so if you plan to breed exhibition birds you will have to band them when the chicks are young. A split band is useful for identification, but does not provide confirmation of breeding origins.

CLOSE-BANDING A CHICK ▷
Slide the closed band over the young chick's three longest toes. Hold the fourth toe back against the leg while you pass the band over it, then release.

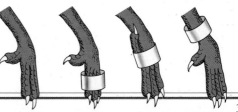

FINCHES

62 ORANGE-CHEEKED WAXBILL

(*Estrilda melpoda*) Easy to look after, though rather shy, these small West African finches prefer to live in a densely planted aviary where they like to nest close to the ground. As they are not completely hardy, keep them indoors until all danger of frost has passed. These birds usually prove compatible with other waxbills of similar size, but avoid boisterous companions who may interfere with the birds' nesting activities. Feed these birds on a standard foreign-finch seed mix, supplemented with a selection of green food and invertebrates.

Characteristic orange cheek plumage appears in chicks around six weeks

Red plumage on rump is unique to Orange-cheeked Waxbill

Color of bill resembles that of sealing wax, hence name "waxbill"

Cock bird flicks tail back and forth when displaying to mate

CHARACTERISTICS
Length: 4 in (10 cm)
Average life expectancy: 4 years
Sexing: Visually difficult; hens may be paler with smaller orange cheek patches
Type of nest: Nest or nestbox
Incubation: 12 days
Fledging: 21 days later

63 GOULDIAN FINCH

(Chloebia gouldiae) As well as the two head colors shown here, there is also a black-headed form of this brilliantly colored bird; lilac- and white-breasted forms are bred in all three head colors. Pairs do not always breed readily, but you can improve the chance of success by employing Bengalese Finches as foster parents for the eggs and chicks. Natives of Australia, these birds are sensitive to low temperatures, so house them in an indoor flight and feed on a good foreign-finch mix with the addition of a little niger seed.

Tip of cock's bill turns cherry red just before nesting

RED-HEADED COCK

Red-headed form is dominant to black-headed form

YELLOW-HEADED COCK

Vivid purple breast found in all three mutations

Green back and yellow underparts

Short tail with two long, pointed feathers

CHARACTERISTICS
Length: 5 in (12.5 cm)
Average life expectancy: 7 years
Sexing: Hens are paler than cocks
Type of nest: Nestbox in breeding cage
Incubation: 15 days
Fledging: 21 days later

64 ZEBRA FINCH

(*Poephilia guttata*) Easy to breed and raise, Zebra Finches are available in a wide range of color forms including fawn, chestnut-flanked white, silver, and cream. House Zebra Finches in a small outdoor aviary but, if you live in a temperate area, provide additional lighting and warmth in the winter. Feed them on a mixture of millets and canary seed, supplemented by soft foods and green food, especially during the breeding period.

Hen's plumage is duller than that of cock

Cock has red bill and orange cheek patches

Black stripes on breast identify cock bird

No markings on flanks

Hen has no barring on breast

White underparts of this variety give rise to its name "Penguin." (Cock birds have no barring, even on chest, but retain orange cheek patches)

CHARACTERISTICS
Length: 4 in (10 cm)
Average life expectancy: 5 years
Sexing: Barring present on cocks in many cases; hens' bills are paler red
Type of nest: Basket or box
Incubation: 13 days
Fledging: 18 days later

FAWN
PENGUIN
HEN

Ocher coloration
extends around
neck, with darker
shade on chest

65 PARADISE WHYDAH

(*Vidua paradisaea*) Also
known as widow birds
because of the cock's black
plumage, these birds belong to
the whydah group of finches,
which is characterized by the
spectacular breeding plumage
of the cock birds.

Paradise Whydahs do not
rear their own chicks; instead,
the hen usually lays her eggs
in the nest of the Melba
Finch who hatches
the eggs and rears
the chicks. House
Paradise Whydahs
in a large planted
aviary or in a
spacious
indoor
flight.

Tail held almost
horizontally in flight.
Long plumes are
easily damaged, so
provide plenty of
space around perches

Hen has duller
plumage than cock
and no tail plumes

CHARACTERISTICS
Length: 5 in (13 cm)
Average life expectancy:
10 years
Sexing: Hens have duller
plumage and no tail
plumes
Type of nest: Eggs
laid in nest of other finch
Incubation: 14 days
Fledging: 14 days later

Plumes may
be nearly
10 in (25 cm)
long

43

66 NAPOLEON WEAVER

(*Euplectes afra*) Once they are properly acclimatized, these birds can be kept outdoors in winter in temperate areas but they do need a snug shelter in colder weather. Feed on a diet of foreign-finch mix plus green food and insects. To encourage nesting, plant stands of bamboo in the aviary. Be sure to select a variety that will not grow too tall.

Cock has yellow head and breast

CHARACTERISTICS
Length: 5 in (12.5 cm)
Average life expectancy: 7 years
Sexing: Hens have heavier streaking than cocks out of color
Type of nest: Nest, in a colony
Incubation: 14 days
Fledging: 15 days later

Black underparts when in color

67 BENGALESE FINCH

(*Lonchura domestica*) The Bengalese Finch does not occur in the wild, and is believed to be the result of selective crossbreeding, in China, many centuries ago. Available in various forms, including fawn, white, and chocolate, these are among the most popular of finches and are highly valued as foster parents. They are quite hardy and will happily share an aviary with waxbills and other smaller finches.

Fawn and white cock fans tail feathers in breeding display

Markings vary from bird to bird

CHARACTERISTICS
Length: 4 in (10 cm)
Average life expectancy: 5 years
Sexing: Cocks sing, especially at start of breeding season
Type of nest: Nestbox
Incubation: 12 days
Fledging: 21 days later

68 RED-CHEEKED CORDON BLEU

(*Uraeginthus bengalus*) These finches need careful management, but eventually settle down in the right surroundings. They dislike cold and damp and will do well in spacious indoor quarters. If you prefer, keep them in a well-planted, sheltered outdoor aviary in warm weather, but if it is cold you must provide adequate heat and lighting. Feed them on a foreign-finch mix, supplemented by fresh seedheads, soaked seed, and small live food. To help settle newly acquired birds, offer nectar in a sealed fountain. Live food is essential for rearing chicks.

Red cheek patch identifies cock bird. Yellow cheek patches occur occasionally

▽ **BLUE-CAPPED CORDON BLEU**
Sometimes known as the Blue-capped Waxbill, this variety can be sexed easily, as hens have brown heads.

Cock's plumage more brightly colored than hen's

Cock bird has blue head and chest, with no red cheek patch

CHARACTERISTICS
Length: 5 in (12.5 cm)
Average life expectancy: 8 years
Sexing: Hens of all species are paler than cocks
Type of nest: Nest or nesting basket
Incubation: 12 days
Fledging: 21 days later

CANARIES

69 BORDER FANCY CANARY

(*Serinus canaria*) Available in many color varieties, including white, cinnamon, and green, these birds are lively and easy to care for. As they are hardy, they can be kept in an outdoor aviary. Provide them with canary seed mix and a good supply of green food such as spinach, which contains a yellow coloring agent.

CHARACTERISTICS
Length: 5½ in (14 cm)
Average life expectancy: 10 years
Sexing: Cocks sing
Type of nest: Nest pan
Incubation: 14 days
Fledging: 14 days later

Rounded chest and back

70 GLOSTER FANCY CANARY

(*Serinus canaria*) Shown for the first time in 1925, these birds are now widely available. The crest is compact and, unlike that of other canaries, does not extend over the eyes. Genetic study has shown that the crested form is associated with a lethal factor, so they are always paired to uncrested consorts. Offer a standard canary seed mix, green food, and soft food.

CHARACTERISTICS
Length: 4 in (10 cm)
Average life expectancy: 10 years
Sexing: Cocks sing
Type of nest: Nest pan
Incubation: 14 days
Fledging: 14 days later

Thick neck matches relatively broad head

71 RED FACTOR CANARY

(Serinus canaria) The diet of these birds must be monitored carefully, especially during the molt, in order to retain their red coloring. Avoid green food, egg yolk, and rape seed, which all contain lutein, a yellow coloring agent. Offer instead a diet of groats and niger seed, with grated carrot and a special soft food. To show them at their best, you must use a suitable coloring agent.

Standards may specify proportions of light and dark plumage

VARIEGATED INTENSIVE COCK

Tail and wing tips are much paler than the rest of the body

CHARACTERISTICS
Length: *5 in (12.5 cm)*
Average life expectancy: *10 years*
Sexing: *Cocks sing*
Type of nest: *Nest pan*
Incubation: *14 days*
Fledging: *14 days later*

72 LIZARD CANARY

(Serinus canaria) This old breed is distinguished by the unusual spangled pattern of markings on its back. It is available in a clear and broken cap variety, as well as in a noncapped form. Color-feed exhibition birds, commencing before the molt.

Typical clear oval cap runs from bill to base of skull

CHARACTERISTICS
Length: *5 in (12.5 cm)*
Average life expectancy: *10 years*
Sexing: *Cocks sing, especially at start of breeding season*
Type of nest: *Nest pan*
Incubation: *14 days*
Fledging: *14 days later*

SOFTBILLS

73 ZMEROPS

(*Zosterops palpebrosa*) These attractive birds, known sometimes as "White eyes" because of the distinctive white area around the eyes, are among the most popular of all softbills. Sociable birds, they can be kept safely together with other small birds or in groups.

Zosterops become chilled easily, so do not keep them outside unless their plumage is in good condition. Keep plumage healthy by spraying lightly with tepid water each day, or by providing a shallow bath.

Offer Zosterops a wide range of diced fruit, sprinkled with softbill food. They also need live foods and a nectar solution every day.

Narrow, pointed bill allows bird to peck into fruit and flowers and to catch insects

Characteristic white area around eyes

Many Zosterops are greenish yellow, so it can be difficult to distinguish species in some cases

Provide fresh, supple perches, replacing any that become sticky

CHARACTERISTICS
Length: 5 in (12.5 cm)
Average life expectancy: 10 years
Sexing: Scientific sexing required; cocks sing during breeding period
Type of nest: Nest
Incubation: 14 days
Fledging: 14 days later

74 BLUE-NECKED TANAGER

(*Tangara cyanicollis*) These colorful birds are popular and easy to maintain once established. House tanagers in a planted flight, but in cold weather you must provide heated accommodation. Watch for signs of bullying if you keep them in a group, as some birds may be shier than others.

Provide a varied diet of diced fruit and berries, sprinkled with softbill food. It is also important to supply live food, particularly for a nesting pair. Tanagers, especially recently acquired birds, appreciate nectar. These birds enjoy frequent bathing, which helps keep their plumage immaculate and healthy.

CHARACTERISTICS
Length: 5 in (12.5 cm)
Average life expectancy: 8 years
Sexing: Scientific sexing required
Type of nest: Nest
Incubation: 14 days
Fledging: 20 days later

Wing color varies from pure yellow to greenish yellow

Medium-length tail feathers

Head coloration is characteristic feature

Blue coloring appears on flanks as well as on head

Color of these tanagers varies quite widely

BAY-HEADED TANAGER COCK

75 HARTLAUB'S TOURACO
(Tauraco hartlaubi)

Natives of Africa, these brightly colored softbills need a large flying space in an aviary at least 12 ft (3.6 m) long. Although they can tolerate cold weather, make sure that they roost under cover, because their claws are susceptible to frostbite.

Provide a varied diet of fruit, green food sprinkled with softbill food, and some softbill pellets. Touracos tend to dislike live food.

Broad bill and wide gape enables Touracos to pluck berries and swallow fruit

CHARACTERISTICS
Length: *16 in (40 cm)*
Average life expectancy: *12 years*
Sexing: *Scientific sexing required*
Type of nest: *Nesting platform*
Incubation: *20 days*
Fledging: *28 days later*

Crest varies in shape and coloration between different species

Red wing coloration results from copper-based pigment found only in Touracos

◁ **WHITE-CHEEKED TOURACO**
As the name suggests, this variety has distinctive white patches on its cheeks.

76 WHITE-CRESTED JAY THRUSH

(Garrulax leucolophus) One of the laughing thrush group, this lively bird is an attractive songster. If you plan to keep several birds in a group, watch for signs of bullying as they can be aggressive, especially when breeding. Easy to maintain and hardy once acclimatized, they tend to be happiest when housed in a densely planted aviary. Offer White-crested Jay Thrushes softbill food and softened mynah pellets, as well as diced fruit and seeds. A good supply of live food is vital for rearing purposes: scatter this on the floor so that the parents have to hunt for it. This will help prevent the birds from becoming bored, a condition that can lead them to attack their young.

Crest usually held erect

Black eye stripe; sometimes has brownish tinge

Extent of white plumage does not distinguish sexes

Plumage is predominantly brown, with chestnut areas close to white area of neck

Relatively broad tail feathers

CHARACTERISTICS
Length: 12 in (30 cm)
Average life expectancy: 10 years
Sexing: Scientific sexing required; hens may have smaller, grayer crests
Type of nest: Nest
Incubation: 13 days
Fledging: Occurs 21 days later

77 PEKIN ROBIN

(*Leiothrix lutea*) Members of the thrush family, Pekin Robins are distinguished by the attractive song of the cocks, which is heard mainly in the breeding period. Offer them a little canary seed and soaked millet spray, as well as the usual diet of fruit, invertebrates, and prepared foods. They may need extra warmth in cold weather.

Hens often grayer around lores than cock birds

Yellow throat and breast coloration varies in depth

CHARACTERISTICS
Length: *6 in (15 cm)*
Average life expectancy: *10 years*
Sexing: *Scientific sexing required*
Type of nest: *Nest or nestbox*
Incubation: *Lasts 14 days*
Fledging: *Occurs 14 days later*

Closed wings reveal colors

78 FIRE-TUFTED BARBET

(*Psilopogon pyrolophus*) This bird, being a jungle species, adjusts best in a well-planted aviary, but bring them inside in cold weather as they are not really hardy. Offer fruits and berries every day, plus a low-iron soft food and live food. Always have a dish of clean water available for the birds to bathe.

Hairlike feathers around bill are characteristic

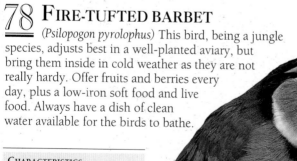

CHARACTERISTICS
Length: *10 in (25 cm)*
Average life expectancy: *8 years*
Sexing: *Scientific sexing required*
Type of nest: *Nestbox or hollow log*
Incubation: *14 days*
Fledging: *20 days later*

Scaling on feet indicates bird's maturity

79 GREATER HILL MYNAH

(Gracula religiosa) The Greater Hill Mynah's remarkable talent for mimicry has guaranteed its continuing popularity. Although relatively hardy, mynahs hate damp, foggy weather and are happier when kept indoors in a large flight unit. Regular bathing is essential for birds housed indoors, to keep their plumage in good condition. It is also important to keep their perches clean to minimize the risk of foot infections. Feed mynahs on diced fruit and softbill food, mynah pellets, and invertebrates.

CHARACTERISTICS
Length: *12 in (30 cm)*
Average life expectancy: *8 years*
Sexing: *Scientific sexing required*
Type of nest: *Nestbox plus nesting material*
Incubation: *14 days*
Fledging: *20 days later*

Bare area of fleshy skin (wattle) more prominent in certain groups of mynah

Black feathering highly iridescent under sunlight, showing purple and green hues

White patch of plumage on flight feathers

BUDGERIGARS

80 DOMINANT PIED BUDGERIGAR

(Melopsittacus undulatus)

Pied budgerigars are distinguished by their variegated markings, with shades of green and yellow or blue and white being the most common combinations. Dominant pieds can be bred easily, because only one member of the pair must be pied in order to produce similar chicks. When there is a broad colored area on the chest, pied budgerigars are described as "banded."

White irises distinguish dominant pieds from recessive mutation

Dominant pieds have three spots on either side of face

◁ LIGHT GREEN DOMINANT PIED

◁ SKY BLUE DOMINANT PIED

Pied markings vary, depending on color. Here, blue coloring predominates

CHARACTERISTICS
Length: 7 in (18 cm)
Average life expectancy: 7 years
Sexing: Hens have brown cere above bill
Type of nest: Nestbox
Incubation: 18 days
Fledging: 35 days later

Dark plum-colored eyes

Even yellow coloration

Flight feathers are paler than on rest of body

81 DARK-EYED YELLOW BUDGERIGAR

(*Melopsittacus undulatus*) This clear yellow budgerigar is distinguished from a lutino by its dark plum-colored eyes. Like other budgerigars, this variety is hardy and can be kept in an aviary throughout the year. Offer a budgerigar seed mix, supplemented with soaked millet spray and soft food when there are chicks in the nest.

CHARACTERISTICS
Length: 7 in (18 cm)
Average life expectancy: 7 years
Sexing: Hens have brown cere above bill
Type of nest: Nestbox
Incubation: 18 days
Fledging: 35 days later

82 CRESTED OPALINE COBALT BUDGERIGAR

(*Melopsittacus undulatus*) There are three crested mutations: full-circular, half-circular, and tufted, all of which can be combined with any color or marking. Good crests are difficult to breed: never pair crested budgies together, but instead pair to normal birds without crests. Before showing, groom the crest with a small brush.

Well-placed flat, even, full-circular crest

CHARACTERISTICS
Length: 7 in (18 cm)
Average life expectancy: 7 years
Sexing: Hens have brown cere above bill
Type of nest: Nestbox
Incubation: 18 days
Fledging: 35 days later

83 GRAY BUDGERIGAR

(*Melopsittacus undulatus*) Only the dominant form of Gray Budgerigar now survives; a separate recessive mutation, which appeared in 1933, became extinct in the 1940s, probably because it reproduced at a slower rate. Color combinations are quite common, including a yellow-faced, a cinnamon, and a white-winged opaline gray form.

Broad head typical of exhibition birds

Clearly defined spots on mask

Gray feet coloration enhances appearance

CHARACTERISTICS
Length: 7 in (18 cm)
Average life expectancy: 7 years
Sexing: Hens have brown cere above bill
Type of nest: Nestbox
Incubation: 18 days
Fledging: Occurs 35 days later

84 LIGHT GREEN BUDGERIGAR

(*Melopsittacus undulatus*) Although this is the natural color form of the budgerigar, specimens found in the wild tend to be much smaller than domesticated birds. They are social birds and live well in groups. Offer a mixture of millets and plain canary seed, green food, and sweet apple. Provide an iodine block to ensure healthy thyroid functioning.

Breast shows palest shade of green coloration; darker shades are also produced

CHARACTERISTICS
Length: 7 in (18 cm)
Average life expectancy: 7 years
Sexing: Hens have brown cere above bill
Type of nest: Nestbox
Incubation: 18 days
Fledging: 35 days later

85 VIOLET RECESSIVE PIED BUDGERIGAR

(*Melopsittacus undulatus*)

One of the smaller varieties, the Recessive Pied Budgerigar can be produced in any of the usual pied combinations, including the darker shades. An unusual feature is that the number of spots in the mask varies and may be completely absent. The mutation originated in Scandinavia and was first exhibited in Denmark in 1932 – hence their common name of Danish Recessive Pieds. They are hardy birds, but if you want to breed them in winter in temperate areas you must provide extra heating and lighting.

CHARACTERISTICS
Length: 7 in (18 cm)
Average life expectancy: 7 years
Sexing: Hens have brown cere above the bill
Type of nest: Nestbox
Incubation: 18 days
Fledging: 35 days later

Dark plum-colored eyes with no clearly evident irises

Pied markings on body vary: usual color is shade of blue and white or green and yellow

Opaline markings mean a relatively pale head coloration

Attractive violet plumage on underparts

◁ OPALINE YELLOW-FACED COBALT
The combination of yellow face and blue body is now a popular variety. The deep brown cere indicates that this is a mature hen budgerigar.

PARAKEETS & COCKATIELS

86 PLUM-HEADED PARAKEET

(Psittacula cyanocephala)

These tolerant and fairly non-destructive parakeets are suitable occupants for a garden aviary in temperate areas. Like most parakeets, they benefit from a long flight. Offer parrot mix with cereal seeds, plus fruit and green food. When seeking a true pair for breeding purposes, check the head of the "hen" for plum-colored feathers, which signify that it is actually a young male.

Plum-colored patch on wing distinguishes this bird from closely related Blossom-headed Parakeet

Characteristic coloration on head acquired over course of several molts

CHARACTERISTICS
Length: 13 in (33 cm)
Average life expectancy: 25 years
Sexing: Hens have gray heads
Type of nest: Nestbox
Incubation: 25 days
Fledging: 50 days later

FEMALE PLUMAGE △
Adult hens are identified by gray heads and absence of plum-colored wing patch.

87 SUN CONURE

(*Aratinga solstitialis*) Although relative newcomers to aviculture, these dazzling birds have proved to be prolific breeders and are now available at reasonable prices. Once acclimatized they are hardy, and can be housed in an outdoor aviary. Feed them on good-quality parrot mix, smaller cereal seeds, plus daily fruit and green food. Provide a nestbox for conures to roost in throughout the year, but replace this with a clean box after the breeding season, to prevent the buildup of parasites.

Body coloration varies between individuals, some being brighter than others

Adults' wings mainly yellow; those of young birds show more green

Body entirely green, apart from head and neck

Extent of red feathering on head depends on individual

MITRED CONURE ▷
(*A. mitrata*) This is one of several species of conure that are mainly green, but with variable amounts of red. Care is the same as for the Sun Conure.

CHARACTERISTICS
Length: 12 in (30 cm)
Average life expectancy: 15 years
Sexing: Scientific sexing required
Type of nest: Nestbox
Incubation: 26 days
Fledging: 56 days later

88 GOLDEN-MANTLED ROSELLA

(*Platycercus eximius*) This colorful species from southeast Australia and Tasmania is a more colorful form of the Eastern Rosella. House them in an outdoor aviary with a 12 ft (3.6 m) flight; feed on canary seed, millets, groats, and sunflower seed, plus green food and apple.

CHARACTERISTICS
Length: 12 in (30 cm)
Average life expectancy: 15 years
Sexing: Hens are duller than cocks, with less red on head and breast
Type of nest: Nestbox
Incubation: 21 days
Fledging: 35 days later

Merging of red and yellow feathering on breast varies from one bird to another

Broad individual tail feathers, even at tip

89 LINEOLATED PARAKEET

(*Bolborhynchus lineola*) These quiet and inoffensive birds from South America are unusual in aviculture. Some mutations are available, including a stunning, but rare, blue variant. Keep them in a secluded aviary, with plenty of cover, as they dislike bright light. They may need additional warmth during very cold weather.

Short, broad tail tapers to fine point

CHARACTERISTICS
Length: 6 in (15 cm)
Average life expectancy: 10 years
Sexing: Scientific sexing required
Type of nest: Nestbox
Incubation: 18 days
Fledging: 35 days later

Black wing markings give rise to other name, Barred Parakeet

90 BLUE RING-NECKED PARAKEET

(Psittacula krameri) Highly valued by Indian rulers centuries ago, this striking mutation is being bred in ever-increasing numbers now. The plumage of cocks and hens is identical except for the distinctive collar that cocks acquire at about three years of age. Offer these hardy birds parrot food, cereal seeds (including groats), fruit, and green food, and house in an aviary. Breed mutations on their own to be certain of the chicks' parentage.

Collar serves to distinguish sexes easily

Depth of blue coloration varies little from one individual to another. Normal coloration of ring-necked parakeets is green

Toes susceptible to frostbite

CHARACTERISTICS
Length: 16 in (40 cm)
Average life expectancy: 15 years
Sexing: Hens lack distinctive collar of cocks
Type of nest: Nestbox
Incubation: 24 days
Fledging: 50 days later

△ FEMALE PLUMAGE
The plumage of hens is identical to that of cocks, except that the former have no neck collar.

91 SPLENDID GRASS PARAKEET

(*Neophema splendida*) Sometimes known as the Scarlet-chested Parakeet, this bird is an ideal choice for newcomers to aviculture, and will become quite tame when housed in an aviary. Offer a basic diet of millets and canary seed, with a little sunflower seed and groats, plus green food and sweet apple.

Relatively large eyes allow bird to be active at dusk

Powerful wings make bird very agile in flight and difficult to catch in aviary

CHARACTERISTICS
Length: 7 in (19 cm)
Average life expectancy: 12 years
Sexing: Cock birds have red breasts
Type of nest: Nestbox
Incubation: 19 days
Fledging: 28 days later

92 RED-FRONTED KAKARIKI

(*Cyanoramphus novaezelandiae*) At one time in danger of extinction in its native New Zealand, this prolific breeder is now widely kept in aviculture. House in an aviary, but be sure to keep the floor clean and dry, as they often scratch around looking for food – a habit that makes them susceptible to roundworms. Offer Kakarikis a diet of budgerigar seed, fruit, and green food, and occasionally mealworms.

Red head markings characterize this species

Predominantly dark green body coloration

CHARACTERISTICS
Length: 11 in (28 cm)
Average life expectancy: 6 years
Sexing: Hens are smaller than cocks
Type of nest: Nestbox
Incubation: 19 days
Fledging: 42 days later

93 COCKATIEL

(*Nymphicus hollandicus*) A native of Australia, and popular in Europe since the 1840s, the Cockatiel has a cheerful disposition that has made it a worldwide favorite with aviculturists. Deworm newly acquired birds before releasing them into the aviary, as they are especially prone to roundworm infestation. Offer Cockatiels a diet of millets and plain canary seed, a little apple, sunflower seeds, and green food.

Crest held more vertically when bird is excited or displaying, as in this case

Hen's facial coloration duller than that of cock

Distinctive yellow and black barring on underside of hen's tail

△ LUTINO COCKATIEL
The lutino has become the most popular color form of the Cockatiel. The darkest lutino birds are sometimes described as "golden" or "buttercup."

CHARACTERISTICS
Length: 12 in (30 cm)
Average life expectancy: 18 years
Sexing: Hens have duller facial coloration than cocks; they also have barring on underside of tails
Type of nest: Nestbox
Incubation: 18 days
Fledging: 28 days later

PARROTS & COCKATOOS

94 PEACH-FACED LOVEBIRD

(*Agapornis roseicollis*) This popular small parrot has been bred in a wide range of colors and makes a delightful pet, especially if hand-reared. It has a less raucous call than other parrots, and may learn to repeat a few words. Offer a basic diet of canary seed, millets, groats, and some sunflower seed, plus a little apple and green food. House these birds in an aviary.

Red eye

LUTINO
PEACH-FACED
LOVEBIRD

Eye ring less prominent than in some lovebirds

Distinctive short, rounded tail feathers

CHARACTERISTICS
Length: 6 in (15 cm)
Average life expectancy: *10 years*
Sexing: *Scientific sexing required*
Type of nest: *Nestbox*
Incubation: *23 days*
Fledging: *42 days later*

95 AFRICAN GRAY PARROT

(Psittacus erithacus) This bird is an exceptional mimic – a talent that has ensured its great popularity. It is hardy enough to be housed in an aviary in all but the coldest weather, and its plumage will benefit from rain and fresh air, but a bird kept in an aviary will not become tame, especially if acquired as an adult.

Yellow eye coloration identifies adult bird

Red tail feathers

CHARACTERISTICS
Length: *13 in (32.5 cm)*
Average life expectancy: *50 years*
Sexing: *Scientific sexing required*
Type of nest: *Nestbox*
Incubation: *29 days*
Fledging: *90 days later*

96 ORANGE-WINGED AMAZON PARROT

(Amazona amazonica) A native of South America, this bird is somewhat similar to the better-known Blue-fronted Amazon Parrot, although it is slightly smaller. House these and other Amazon parrots in a sturdy, spacious aviary or cage and provide plenty of perches for them to gnaw.

Face markings differ from one bird to another

Orange feathering most apparent when wings are open

CHARACTERISTICS
Length: *13 in (33 cm)*
Average life expectancy: *40 years*
Sexing: *Scientific sexing required*
Type of nest: *Nestbox*
Incubation: *27 days*
Fledging: *50 days later*

97 GREEN-WINGED MACAW

(*Ara chloroptera*) These vividly colored large birds from Central and South America can become very tame and pairs usually nest readily. House them indoors or in an outdoor aviary, but make sure that their accommodation is sturdy, and provide an ample supply of branches for them to gnaw on – otherwise they are likely to cause considerable damage with their bills. Offer a basic diet of parrot food, fruit, and green food, and a regular supply of a variety of nuts. Although its call is loud, this species is not given to prolonged screeching bouts.

Macaw's bill is typically large and powerful

Green coloration on wings distinguishes this species from Scarlet Macaw, which has yellow plumage on wings

Long tail feathers may become frayed if perches are positioned too close to sides of aviary

CHARACTERISTICS
Length: *36 in (90 cm)*
Average life expectancy: *50 years*
Sexing: *Scientific sexing required; hens may have smaller heads than cock birds*
Type of nest: *Sturdy nestbox*
Incubation: *28 days*
Fledging: *90 days later*

98 GREEN-NAPED LORIKEET

(Trichoglossus haematodus)

Originating from islands off the coast of Asia, the many forms of Green-naped Lorikeet vary only slightly in their coloration. Keep them outdoors in temperate areas, but always ensure that their quarters are easy to clean as they have messy feeding habits. Offer a diet of nectar solution and dry nectar as well as a selection of diced fresh fruit every day, and some green food and seed, such as soaked millet spray. If you adjust their diet in any way, do so slowly to avoid disturbance of the digestive tract.

CHARACTERISTICS
Length: *11 in (26 cm)*
Average life expectancy:
25 years
Sexing: *Scientific sexing required*
Type of nest: *Sturdy nestbox*
Incubation: *25 days*
Fledging: *Occurs 70 days later*

Barring pattern on body varies according to race

Striated markings on underparts vary slightly between individuals

Subtle color on abdomen contrasts with brighter breast coloration

Red area on forehead present in both sexes

◁ **GOLDIE'S LORIKEET COCK**
(Trichoglossus goldiei) This variety, at 7 in (19 cm) long, is ideal for a small aviary. It may need extra heat in cold weather. As with many lories and lorikeets, these birds breed readily.

99 CELESTIAL PARROTLET

(*Forpus coelestis*) These lively little parrots are an ideal choice if your space is limited, as they can be housed in a cage or small aviary. They are aggressive to their own kind, so, if you have adjoining pairs in aviaries, separate them with taut double-wiring or a wooden partition. Offer budgerigar seed mix or millets and canary seed with some sunflower seeds, green food, and fruit.

Blue markings on head identify this as cock bird; cock also has blue wing feathering

CHARACTERISTICS
Length: 5 in (12.5 cm)
Average life expectancy: 20 years
Sexing: Hens have duller plumage, and lack blue coloration of cocks
Type of nest: Nestbox
Incubation: 18 days
Fledging: 42 days later

100 CHATTERING LORY

(*Lorius garrulus*) These colorful and lively birds quickly become tame, even when housed in an aviary. Wash or replace their perches regularly, as they become sticky with nectar and droppings. Provide a fresh solution of nectar once or twice a day, along with green food, fruit, and a little seed. Offer mealworms, especially when there are chicks in the nest, as well as a supply of grit.

Yellow patch on back indicates bird belongs to yellow-backed race

CHARACTERISTICS
Length: 12 in (30 cm)
Average life expectancy: 25 years
Sexing: Scientific sexing required
Type of nest: Sturdy nestbox
Incubation: 28 days
Fledging: 70 days later

Feet and claws are gray

101 Umbrella Cockatoo

(Cacatua alba) This spectacular bird, sometimes known as the Great White Cockatoo, is one of the largest of the cockatoos. Once acclimatized, these birds are hardy and stay outdoors in temperate areas, but their very loud, penetrating calls may annoy neighbors.

They need a strong aviary to withstand damage from their powerful bills – try to deflect their destructive attentions by providing a supply of soft wood pieces for them to chew. Offer parrot mixture, fruit, green food, and pellets, although they may not be eager to eat these.

Broadly shaped crest gives rise to name Umbrella Cockatoo

Grayish colored feet contrast with white plumage

Eye ring consists of bare area of white skin

Characteristics
Length: 12 in (30 cm)
Average life expectancy: 40 years
Sexing: Hens usually have dark reddish brown eye coloration
Type of nest: Sturdy nestbox
Incubation: 28 days
Fledging: 80 days later

INDEX

ACKNOWLEDGMENTS

Dorling Kindersley would like to thank Hilary Bird for compiling the index, Mark Bracey for computer assistance, Ann Kay for proofreading, and Max Sanderson, Southern Aviaries.

Photography
KEY: t *top*; b *bottom*; c *center*; l *left*; r *right*
All photographs by Cyril Laubscher except for:
Paul Bricknell 4, 7, 11l, 12tl, 13tl, 13tr, 14, 15t, 16tr, 16bc, 16br, 17cl, 17bl, 18, 20tr, 20br, 22tl, 22tc, 22tr, 22cl, 23bl, 23br, 24bc, 25tl, 25br, 26tl, 26cl, 26cr, 26cc, 27br, 29, 30, 31, 32, 36tr, 39tl, 39cl, 46t; Peter Chadwick 33cl, 38cc, 38cr; Andy Crawford 15br, 24, 25, 27, 35cc, 35cr, 35br, 38cl, 38bc, 38br; Colin Keates 26br; Dave King 19tr.

Illustrations
All illustrations by Hardlines, Oxford.